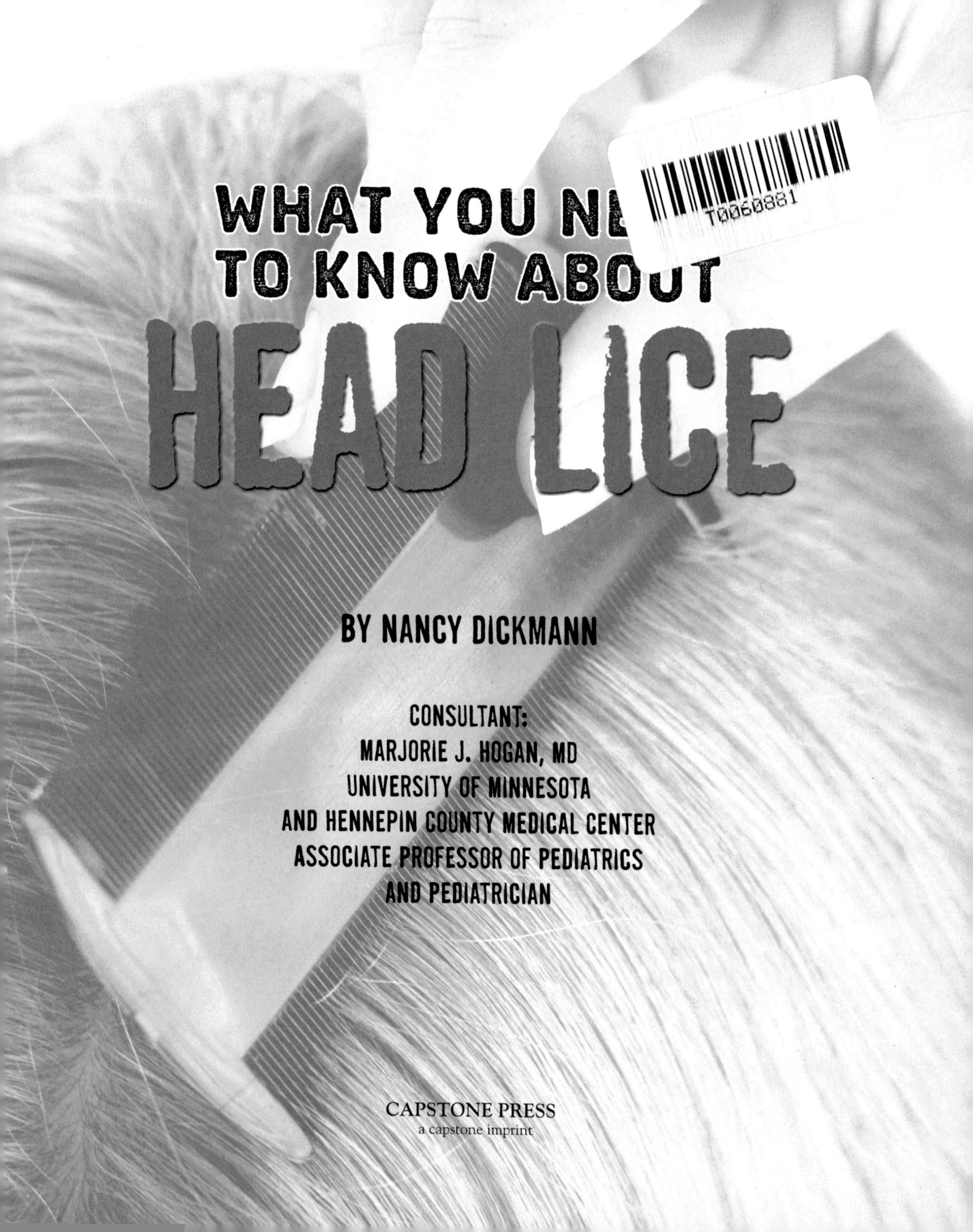

WHAT YOU NEED TO KNOW ABOUT
HEAD LICE

BY NANCY DICKMANN

CONSULTANT:
MARJORIE J. HOGAN, MD
UNIVERSITY OF MINNESOTA
AND HENNEPIN COUNTY MEDICAL CENTER
ASSOCIATE PROFESSOR OF PEDIATRICS
AND PEDIATRICIAN

CAPSTONE PRESS
a capstone imprint

Fact Finders Books are published by Capstone Press,
1710 Roe Crest Drive, North Mankato, Minnesota 56003
www.mycapstone.com

Library of Congress Cataloging-in-Publication Data
Names: Dickmann, Nancy, author.
Title: What you need to know about head lice / by Nancy Dickmann.
Other titles: Fact finders. Focus on health.
Description: North Mankato, Minnesota : Capstone Press, a Capstone imprint,
    [2017] | Series: Fact finders. Focus on health | Audience: Ages 8-11. |
    Audience: Grades 4 to 6. | Includes bibliographical references and index.
Identifiers: LCCN 2015045749 |
ISBN 9781491482421 (library binding) |
ISBN 9781491482469 (paperback) |
ISBN 9781491482506 (eBook PDF)
Subjects: LCSH: Pediculosis—Juvenile literature. |
    Pediculosis—Treatment—Juvenile literature. | Lice—Juvenile literature.
Classification: LCC RL764.P4 D53 2017 | DDC 616.5/72—dc23
LC record available at http://lccn.loc.gov/2015045749

Produced by Brown Bear Books Ltd.
Editor: Tracey Kelly
Design Manager: Keith Davis
Editorial Director: Lindsey Lowe
Children's Publisher: Anne O'Daly
Picture Manager: Sophie Mortimer
Production Manager: Alastair Gourlay

Photo Credits
Front Cover: Shutterstock: (top); Science Photo Library: Power and Syred (bottom).
Inside: 1, © Thinkstock/Stockbyte. 3, © Shutterstock/A N Protatsov. 4 (bottom), © Shutterstock. 5, © Science Photo Library/ Dr Chris Hale. 6 (center), © FLPA/Albert Lleal/Minden Pictures. 6 (bottom right), © Science Photo Library/Stev Gschmeissner. 7, © Shutterstock: Vadim Bukharin. 8, © Science Photo Library/Eye of Science. 9 (top), © Shutterstock/A N Protatsov. 10, © Science Photo Library/Eye of Science. 11, © Science Photo Library/Eye of Science. 12, © Shutterstock/Samuel Borges Photography. 13, © HeadLiceGirlsBainbridge. 14, © Shutterstock. 15 (left), © Thinkstock/istockphoto. 15 (right), © Thinkstock/Jose Elias. 16, © Thinkstock/istockphoto. 17, © Shutterstock: Spotmatick Ltd. 18, © Shutterstock/Monkey Business images. 19, © Amazon. 21, © Thinkstock/Justin Cleary; 22, © Thinkstock/Mike Watson Images; 23, © Getty Images: Mediator Medical; 24, © Thinkstock/ Laura Cruise. 25 (top), © Thinkstock/istockphoto. 25 (center), © Shutterstock/Lopolo. 26, © Shutterstock: Sergey Novikov. 27, © Shutterstock: O M Oliver. 28, © Thinkstock/Stretch Photography. 29, © Dreamstime/Monkey Business Images.

007686WKTF16

Printed in China

TABLE OF CONTENTS

CHAPTER 1
WHAT ARE HEAD LICE?

One morning, you might notice that your head feels tickly or itchy. You may then develop a rash just behind your ears or on the back of your neck. What could be causing these **symptoms**? There are many conditions that could cause an itchy **scalp**, but one possible reason is that some unwelcome visitors have decided to make you their home! These creatures are called head lice.

▼ Head lice can make your head itch.

▲ It's hard to see nits and head lice just by looking at your hair.

Head lice are tiny insects that can live on a person's head. They are big enough to see without a **microscope**, but even so, you might not notice that you have them. Sometimes they can cause your scalp to itch, but many people feel no itching at all. Even so, most people who get head lice go through treatment to get rid of them.

symptom—something different you notice about your body, suggesting that there is an illness or a health problem

scalp—the skin on the top and back of the head, which is usually covered by hair

microscope—scientific tool for looking at very small objects

LOOKING AT HEAD LICE

Adult head lice are small and flat—about the size of the sesame seeds you may see on a bagel. Their color can range from grayish-white to tan. But they can look darker on people with dark hair or when their stomachs are full of blood. Like all insects, head lice have six legs with clawlike **pincers**. They have a body that is divided into three segments: the head, thorax, and **abdomen**.

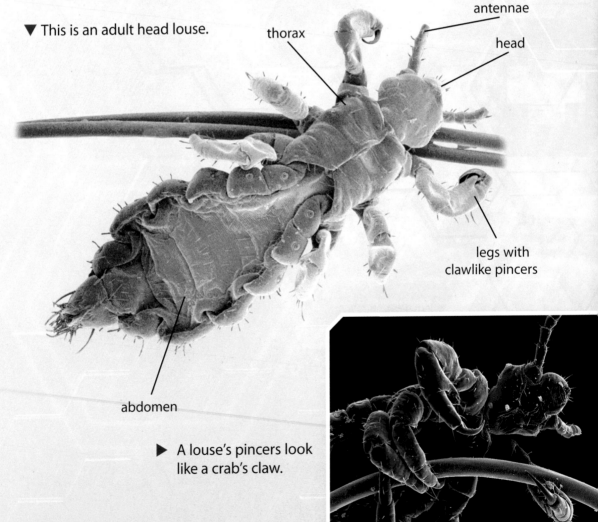

▼ This is an adult head louse.

thorax

antennae

head

legs with clawlike pincers

abdomen

▶ A louse's pincers look like a crab's claw.

Head lice don't have wings, so they can't fly. They aren't good jumpers, either. What they are really good at is clinging. Each of their six short legs has a clawlike pincer at the end. These pincers can grab tightly onto a strand of hair. Lice are also very quick to climb up hair.

HEALTH FACT

There are many different **species** of louse, and the ones that live on humans don't live on any other animals. A closely related species lives on chimpanzees. Other species make their homes on other types of mammals and birds.

◄ Dogs can get lice—but not the same kind as humans get.

pincer—a body part with two pieces that squeeze together to hold or grab something

abdomen—the bottom segment of an insect's body

species—a group of living things that can mate with one another and produce fertile offspring

LOUSE LIFE CYCLE

A louse starts its life cycle by hatching from an egg. The eggs are called nits, and they look like tiny white cylinders. A female head louse lays her eggs close to a person's scalp, where it is nice and warm. Each egg is stuck firmly to a strand of hair. When the eggs hatch one to two weeks later, the empty eggshells stay stuck to the hair.

A baby head louse is called a **nymph**. Its shape is similar to an adult's but smaller. It feeds on human blood and grows bigger. When it grows too big for its hard outer skin, it sheds it. This happens three times before the louse is an adult. The whole process, from hatching to adulthood, takes just over a week.

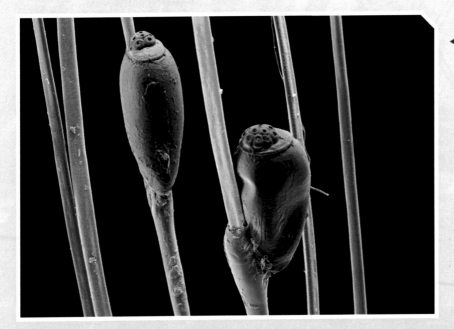

◀ The egg is inside a sac that sticks to the hair.

▶ A nymph's abdomen is smaller than an adult's.

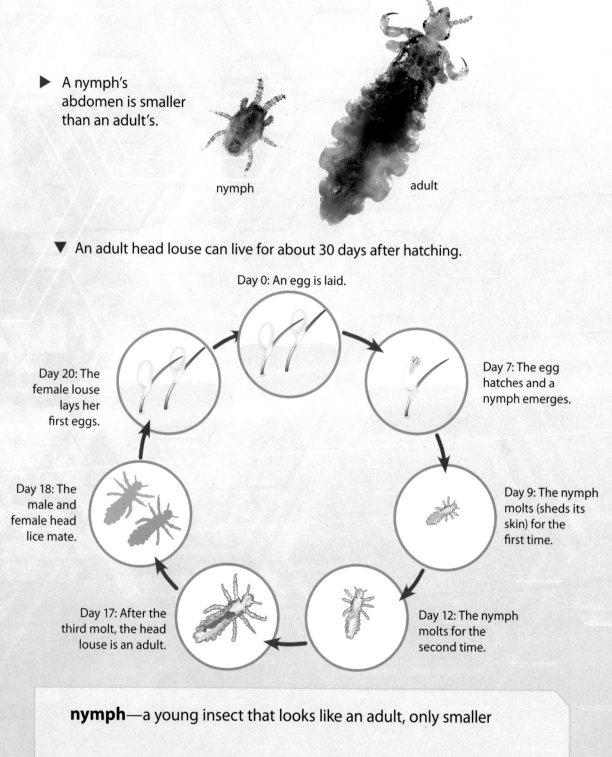

nymph

adult

▼ An adult head louse can live for about 30 days after hatching.

Day 0: An egg is laid.

Day 7: The egg hatches and a nymph emerges.

Day 9: The nymph molts (sheds its skin) for the first time.

Day 12: The nymph molts for the second time.

Day 17: After the third molt, the head louse is an adult.

Day 18: The male and female head lice mate.

Day 20: The female louse lays her first eggs.

nymph—a young insect that looks like an adult, only smaller

FEEDING

Once a head louse has hatched from its egg, it must find food. Head lice eat only one thing: human blood. A head louse will die in just one or two days if it leaves its host and cannot get any blood to eat. Because they live off another living thing, lice are **parasites**.

▼ A louse uses its legs and pincers to crawl toward the scalp to feed.

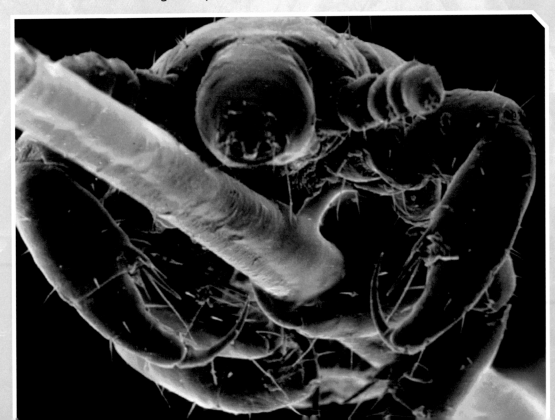

A louse has its first meal within 24 hours of hatching. By the time it is an adult, it will feed several times a day. The amount of blood that a louse takes is very small, so it won't hurt you. After a meal, when its abdomen is full of blood, a louse may look slightly darker. It can also leave reddish-brown droppings on your scalp.

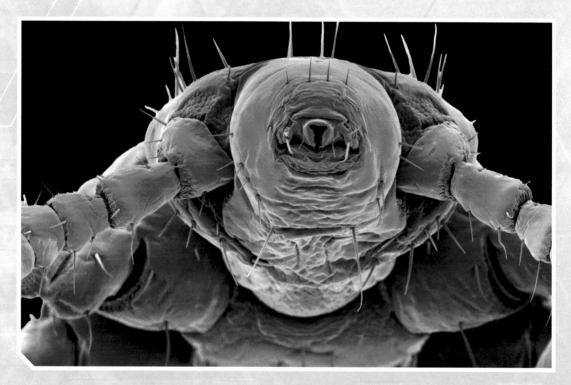

▲ Head lice feed on blood within 24 hours of hatching.

parasite—a plant or animal that lives on another living thing and gets its food and energy from it

saliva—a clear liquid produced by your mouth (sometimes called spit)

CHAPTER 2
FINDING HEAD LICE

Some people who have head lice will have an itchy scalp, but other people will feel nothing at all. The itching is not caused by the head lice biting the scalp. Instead, an **allergy** to their saliva makes the scalp itch. Not everyone is allergic to head lice, which is why some people can have them without itching.

▼ You may not even notice if you have head lice.

Ryan didn't have an itchy head, but when his mom was combing his hair one morning, she saw what looked like tiny eggs. The school nurse confirmed that these were nits. When she found that he also had live lice, she told Ryan's mom that Ryan needed some treatment.

Even for people who are allergic to lice, it may take up to three months for itching to start. Other symptoms of head lice include a tickling feeling in your hair. You may also have trouble sleeping, since lice are most active at night.

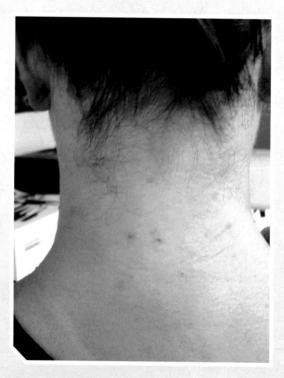

▶ A rash caused by head lice. Not everyone who has head lice gets a rash.

allergy—a condition that makes your body react to certain things, such as pollen or certain foods. An allergy can cause itching, rashes, or other problems

WHAT TO LOOK FOR

The only way to be sure if you have head lice is to find a live adult or nymph in your hair. Unfortunately, they are small and they move quickly, so they are hard to spot. They also avoid light, so when you part your hair to check, they will scurry to a safer spot. An adult can comb through your hair to check for lice using a special fine-tooth comb.

▲ Sometimes you can see head lice just by looking, but you need to use a special detector comb to be sure.

▶ There are different types of lice detection combs. You can buy a lice detection comb at a pharmacy.

Searching for Head Lice

You can search for head lice in dry hair, but it is easier to find lice if your hair is wet. This is because the lice can't move so well then. Combing your wet hair with lots of conditioner on makes it even more likely that you will find any lice that are there.

CHAPTER 3
TREATING HEAD LICE

If you find a live louse when combing your hair, then you definitely have head lice. If you find only nits, especially ones that are not right next to the scalp, it may mean that you did have head lice, but they are now gone. You should still comb carefully to be sure.

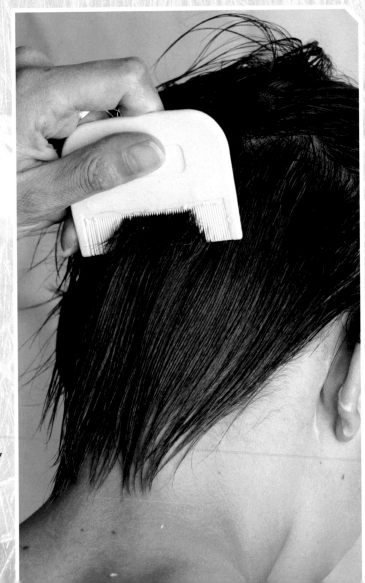

▶ You may want to comb wet hair every week to check for head lice, especially if other children at your school have them.

▲ Children often pass lice on to their brothers, sisters, and parents.

If you have head lice, then you will need to go through treatment to get rid of them. There are many different ways of treating head lice, and they won't hurt you. It may take several treatments before the head lice are all gone.

Head lice can be passed from one person to another. So when someone in your family finds a live louse on his or her head, then everyone in the family should be checked. However, only the family members who definitely have lice should have treatment.

SHAMPOOS AND CREAM RINSES

Many people treat head lice with a special shampoo or cream rinse. These can be bought at a pharmacy or prescribed by your doctor. There are many types, so your parent must always follow the instructions that come with the product.

HEALTH FACT

Some types of head lice shampoo only kill nymphs and adults. Other types kill the eggs too. If you are using a shampoo that doesn't kill eggs, you will need to shampoo again about a week later. This will kill any eggs that have had a chance to hatch since then.

▲ Your doctor can give you advice about treating head lice.

▲ Some types of lice treatment have to be left on for a while before rinsing them out over a sink.

Your parent will usually leave the shampoo or cream rinse in for a while before washing it out. Then he or she can comb any lice (either alive or dead) out of your hair with a fine-tooth comb. You'll need to check for lice every few days to make sure they're all gone.

WET COMBING

Some people don't like the idea of using medicated shampoos and other lice removal products that contain chemicals. There are more natural ways of treating head lice, although they don't always work as well. Wet combing is often used. To work correctly, wet combing needs to be done often and carefully, using the right equipment. It can take time to do, especially if your hair is long or curly.

Some people use natural plant oils to treat head lice. These include tea tree oil, anise oil, and ylang-ylang oil. Some people also put greasy substances, such as mayonnaise, olive oil, and butter, on their hair and leave it overnight. However, there is no scientific evidence that these treatments really work to get rid of head lice. Doctors do not recommend their use.

How to Wet Comb

- Wash hair and apply plenty of ordinary hair conditioner.
- Use a regular comb to straighten and untangle the hair.
- Switch to a special detection comb, and start combing, making sure to start at the scalp.
- Comb to the end of the hair, and then check the comb for lice.
- Wipe or rinse the comb to get rid of any lice.
- Work through all the hair, section by section.
- Rinse out the conditioner, and then repeat the combing.
- Repeat this process on days 3, 6, 9, 12, and 15 to catch newly hatched lice.

◀ Combing wet hair regularly with a special comb can help get rid of head lice.

ALEX'S STORY

Alex had head lice. Her mom washed Alex's hair and put lots of her favorite conditioner in it. She then carefully combed Alex's hair little by little with a special comb. Alex has long hair, so it took half an hour to do!

GETTING RID OF LICE

Sometimes getting rid of the lice on your head isn't enough. Lice can live for 24 to 48 hours away from a human head. If you've used bedding, clothes, or hats within that time and before treatment, wash them on a hot setting. Head lice will die if the temperature is high enough.

HEALTH FACT

Remember that head lice will die without blood to eat. They cannot live for long away from a human head. Although someone in your family may have head lice, the lice are unlikely to survive long on carpets or furniture.

▲ Washing clothes and bed linen in hot water is a simple way to kill any lice or eggs.

An adult should treat combs and hairbrushes by soaking them in very hot water for several minutes. If you need to treat something that can't be washed, seal it in a plastic bag. Leave the bag for two weeks. Any lice that are on it will die in that time, including eggs. Toys such as stuffed animals can be treated in this way.

◀ Head lice could crawl onto your toys if you keep them in bed with you.

CHAPTER 4

PREVENTING HEAD LICE

Head lice cannot jump, swim, or fly. The most common way that they are spread is when the head of someone with lice touches someone else's. This could happen when playing, taking part in sports, or sleeping close together. Head lice are often passed from one student to another at school.

◀ A head louse can quickly crawl from one person's head to another.

It's better not to share hats or scarves with your friends. ◄

Head lice can also be spread by sharing items such as hats, scarves, coats, hair accessories, or hairbrushes. However, this does not happen as often. You cannot catch head lice from a pet, such as a dog or cat.

▲ Even if you have head lice, you can't pass them on to your pet.

TAYLOR'S STORY

Taylor had had head lice for months. Before long, she passed them on to her younger sister. Their dad found lice when he was combing their hair one day. He used a special medicated cream rinse on their hair. He repeated the treatment seven days later, and the lice were destroyed.

NO NITS HERE!

Anyone can catch head lice. It doesn't matter how old you are, how long your hair is, or how often you wash it. There is no kind of pill, shot, or shampoo that can keep you from getting head lice. Luckily, although the lice may make you itch, they won't make you ill.

▲ Don't let head lice keep you from having fun!

The main way that lice spread is through head-to-head contact, when a louse crawls from one head to another. If you lie down with someone make sure there is space between your pillows. If you share a pillow or your heads touch, you may pass on head lice.

▶ You can catch head lice by lying close together at a slumber party.

Remember!

- Lots of people get head lice at some time. It's very common.
- It's good to have your hair checked for head lice regularly.
- There's no need for you to stay home from school if you have head lice.
- Don't avoid people with head lice. You can't catch head lice unless your heads touch for a while.
- There's lots of advice available for dealing with head lice. Ask your school nurse or doctor.

FACT OR FICTION?

There are a lot of **myths** about head lice. Some people think that having lice means that you are dirty, but this is not true. Other people will tell you that head lice only like clean hair, but this is not true, either. Head lice can live on all types of hair: short or long, straight or curly, clean or dirty.

HEALTH FACT

Some people believe that head lice spread disease. Other biting insects, such as mosquitoes, can spread disease, but head lice can't. They are annoying rather than harmful.

▲ Head lice nest in all types of hair, no matter what it looks like!

In the past, parents sometimes shaved their children's heads if they had lice. But this doesn't help. Lice can still live on very short hair. Other parents kept their children home from school. But head lice are less **contagious** than many common illnesses, such as colds and flu. Having head lice is no reason to skip school!

▲ There is no need to stay home from school if you have head lice.

myth—a story or idea that is made up and not real
contagious—able to be passed on from one person to another

GLOSSARY

abdomen (AB-doh-men)—the bottom segment of an insect's body

allergy (A-ler-jee)—a condition that makes your body react to certain things, such as pollen or certain foods. An allergy can cause itching, rashes, or other problems.

contagious (kun-TAY-jus)—able to be passed on from one person to another

microscope (MY-kroh-skope)—scientific tool for looking at very small objects

myth (MITH)—a story or idea that is made up and not real

nymph (NIMF)—a young insect that looks like an adult, only it is smaller

parasite (PAIR-uh-sight)—a plant or animal that lives on another living thing and gets its food and energy from it

pincer (PIN-sir)—a body part with two pieces that squeeze together to hold or grab something

saliva (suh-LIE-vuh)—a clear liquid produced by your mouth (sometimes called spit)

scalp (SKALP)—the skin on the top and back of the head, which is usually covered by hair

species (SPEE-sheez)—a group of living things that can mate with one another and produce fertile offspring

symptom (SIMP-tum)—something different you notice about your body, suggesting that there is an illness or health problem

READ MORE

Fromer, Liza, and Francine Gerstein. *My Itchy Body*. Body Works. Toronto, Ontario: Tundra Books, 2012.

Gravel, Elise. *Head Lice*. Disgusting Creatures. Plattsburg, N.Y.: Tundra Books, 2015.

Huey, Lois Miner. *Ick! Yuck! Eew!: Our Gross American History*. Minneapolis: 21st Century, 2013.

Rath, Tracy. *Louse Out: Every Kid's Self-Help Guide to the 11-Day Process of Getting Head Lice Out of Their Hair*. San Marcos, Calif.: Get Branded Press, 2015.

Royston, Angela. *Itches and Scratches*. Disgusting Body Facts. Chicago: Heinemann-Raintree, 2010.

INTERNET SITES

FactHound offers a safe, fun way to find Internet sites related to this book. All of the sites on FactHound have been researched by our staff.

Here's all you do:

Visit *www.facthound.com*

Type in this code: 9781491482421

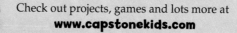

Super-cool stuff! Check out projects, games and lots more at **www.capstonekids.com**

INDEX